Berkley

TRAVELING TOGETHER

The All-Inclusive Guide to Traveling and Vacationing With Children

Authors: Shiela H. Leon
Editor: Emily Roller
Designer: Francesca Guido

Visit us @ www.theflyingkids.com

Contact us: leonardo@theflyingkids.com

ISBN: 978-1500381080

TRAVELING TOGETHER
The All-Inclusive Guide to Traveling and Vacationing With Children

Table of Contents

Introduction

Your children are the most important people in your life. You worry about them constantly: are you feeding them right? Are they getting enough rest? Are your parenting skills on par? You had no idea being a parent would be so life affirming and yet so, so scary. You long to give your children all the beautiful things in the world, and thus you scrimp and scheme: you decide you'll take them on a family vacation they'll never forget. Surely it'll be relaxing: a marvelous vacation for all of you, no matter your age.

You begin by looking at vacation through rose-tinted glasses. You remember your family vacations growing up with your own parents. You have those awkward, tinted photos of you in front of the Disney World castle, chocolate ice cream plastered across your face. Those were brilliant times, you remember.

But now that you've grown up and created a family of your own, you begin to see the flaws in your memory. You begin to understand that the reason your vacations were so wonderful was because your parents had to work and plan it that way. You realize there are about a million things to consider: first of all, where will you go? And how will you get there? How are your parents smiling in those old photos? Traveling is stressful!

Traveling Together - The All-Inclusive Guide to Traveling and Vacationing With Children forces you to look at the facts of fun. It lends you the secrets behind what your children really want in a vacation: babies want to be cuddled and bottled, of course, but what does your sixteen-year-old really need from your trip? And how do you juggle everyone's various ideas of vacation without disappointing someone you love?

Take the focused questionnaire included in this guide in order to rectify your destination dilemmas, and analyze your results. You may be surprised at your options: the world is, after all, quite large. There's a vacation for every personality and every family.

Your family's personality and budget may lead you down the road for a stay-cation; this guide allows you to understand the ways in which you can make your own town sparkle in the safety of the cost-friendly city limits. You can scrape off your day-to-day routines and see a different side of the world in which you inhabit. A stay-cation requires an active imagination, an eager sense of adventure, and complete cooperation. Stopping at the office, for example, is strictly prohibited.

Your family may yearn for a vacation in the realms of a different city or a different country. This guide allows you to understand the proper ways to budget each day of that vacation; it outlines the three areas of vacation cost: transportation, accommodation, and, of course, fun. Be warned: different countries have different conversion rates. Fun might cost a little more in Paris than it does in Smalltown, U.S.A. It's best to watch your pocketbook to avoid any heartbreak when you return.

But this guide's focus, essentially, is to plan a wonderful, happy vacation with your children. It teaches you to work together with them to create a magical few days together. Things will go wrong; you know they always do with kids. But with this guidebook's information in tow you'll understand how to fight back against vacation confusion, culture shock, and strange transportation. You'll understand how to take a pack of kids through a crowded airport and make it out alive, without screams.

You can give your children the life affirming memories you retain from your childhood. Their excitement to learn about the world around them, to reach out and play in new environments, is in your hands. Spice up your every day, lifeless routine, and demonstrate the joys of organized travel. Someday, looking at their own vacation photos, your children will appreciate the hard work and preparation.

In addition to this wonderful book, our online resources at www.theflyingkids.com will offer you an interactive experience with other parents who travel with kids. With lots of blogs, forums for communication, and tips and tricks that they share, The Flying Kids website will prove to be an invaluable resource when used in conjunction with this book.

Chapter 1

The 3 Keys to an Ultimate Family Vacation

We believe that if you pay close attention to our 3-key formula, your family's vacation will not only be optimally planned, but optimally enjoyed as well.

Set your expectations straight. Engage the entire family while you're at it. And prepare for the ideal vacation.

Expectations help you ascertain where you will go and what you will do. Since you're not traveling alone, it should be a given that the whole family needs to come together, and identify what they want from a vacation. Complete relaxation and beach fun, or lots of thrills and adrenaline rush? The more people there are in your family unit, the more ideas will spring up. The key is to discuss, talk and come up with a vacation that satiates everybody's expectations. To that end, we have developed a questionnaire to help you come up with a vacation spot that will keep the whole bunch happy.

Preparations are the stepping stone for any vacation. Thanks to the internet, preparations are now not only a breeze, but loads of fun too. And in the process of setting up the perfect vacation, you get to book travel and accommodations giving yourself the much needed safety net once you set out to capture a new domain, a new territory, a new city. The better prepared you are, the more you'll be able to relax on vacations.

Your preparations must also include a budget, an expected list of expenses, and an itinerary to help you cover all the must-sees and must-dos!

You must also be prepared for the unexpected. This is especially importance with children in tow.

Engagement is a useful quotient to pump up everybody. Lest your teenager or young, observant child feels left out during the planning process, give them a prominent task while you're prepping. You've talked about expectations. You've decided where you want to be. You've made all the preparations. Now get everybody geared up and ready to go. And what better way to do it than to engage with the culture you're headed towards, while you're still at home. This keeps the culture shock to a minimum and the excitement barometer to a maximum. You and the kids could learn some of the foreign language, some of the customs and traditions, maybe stumble upon an exciting festival taking place...you've now never been more ready to set the ball rolling!

Chapter 2

The Definition of Vacation:
Why Your Earnest Family Holiday Planning May Not Have Kids in Mind

Kids are tricky. You know this, of course, from your nightly dining rituals. Your three year old will eat nothing but macaroni and cheese while your thirteen year old is going through a vegan phase. You, on the other hand, would kill for some peace and quiet, maybe an entire bottle of wine to console your rocky, rough—but overall joyful—lifestyle. Ah, yes: the pitfalls and giant, happy mountains of family life.

Kids' school breaks ignite the fire beneath you. You want to go on a family vacation. It'll be great, you think, to scurry away from your safe realm and find something different in the world. You imagine lifting your children's spirits and allowing them to think differently. Maybe this trip will boost their creativity. Maybe you'll finally feel inner solace. Maybe your family will come together as a unit, finally, instead of four or five opinion-oriented, loving and hating, and hugging and hitting personalities.

Unfortunately, you're in for a surprise.

With each distinct age comes a different personality and thus, a different idea of what a vacation really means.

Baby's First Vacation
Your baby's needs must be met throughout each stage of your vacation. There is a silver lining to traveling with small babies: they

are portable. Oh, aren't they portable. As irritating as it can be trying to push a stroller down a crowded, cobblestone alleyway, it's best to take solace in the fact that they can't run fast down a crowded alleyway without you, surrounded by strangers. Not yet.

And furthermore, your small infant has no real idea of what's going on. He or she could be wrapped up in your baby sling across your chest, staring at the very painting that changed Western civilization's art culture as we know it, and he or she wouldn't take a peep. Your baby won't be arguing or complaining about the various things he or she wants to do that day; your baby will need to eat and to sleep the same amount as he or she is used to at home.

There are several preparations you must do prior to taking your baby on a rollicking, adult-oriented adventure. You should make sure to check up on your baby's vaccinations, and allow him or her to receive a valid check up from a doctor. New territory means new germs; you want to make sure your baby's immune system is a revving engine. Furthermore, it's best to push the limits on your diaper bag. Bring about three bottles, as many diapers as you can stuff, and extra formula. You never know when you'll be stuck somewhere in the realms of traveling; you don't want your baby, so used to his or her feeding schedule, to suffer and feel weak because of your ill preparation. Also, remember to bring a bit of blue electric tape. No matter where you are, you'll

want to baby proof some outlets.

In the days before you had an infant, you could do whatever you wanted. You could stay out all night and run around all day. With your infant, your crazy traveling aspects must be tuned down a notch. Now, you can sleep only when your baby sleeps and you can eat only when your baby eats; your body will thank you in the long run.

To summarize:

 The smaller your baby, the more dependant he/she is. Be very prepared whilst traveling.

 Make sure your babies and toddlers are properly vaccinated.

 Pack as much extra diapers, formula and baby food as your luggage will allow.

The Terrible Traveling Toddler's Take on Vacation

Your toddler, on the other hand, will insist that his or her needs be met. Oh boy. Your toddler has opinions. And they so often differ from your own. Your disruptions over the dinner table have nothing on the possible explosions at the beach. At home, you can send your toddler off to steam in his or her room. On vacation, however, you have another battle: you want to retain all the fun and life you've envisioned for your family. But you also can't put up with tantrums.

It's best to try to avoid the pitfalls in the first place. Toddlers don't take well to change, generally, unless it lies in the form of a new toy or a piece of candy. Remember to always narrate whatever you're doing to make your child feel included in the various strange things that are occurring. This is potentially your toddler's first overnight trip away from his or her room. For example, when you're boarding the plane, be sure to acknowledge the strangeness of it all by giving your toddlers the right descriptions in order to push understanding. Tell him or her about the stewardesses, the pilots, and all the other passengers flying to places all over the world. Be sure to be clear and direct. Furthermore, prior to leaving for your destination, describe the place in which you'll be staying to arouse curiosity and excitement in your child. This allows them to look forward to the destination and not to fear it.

Remember when choosing a destination that your toddler doesn't like museums and waiting in line at home; he or she probably won't like museums or waiting in line on vacation either. Be sure to understand that frequent naps are in order; all the extra stimulation will wipe your child out completely. Furthermore, always keep some extra, familiar snacks on hand. Your child will want a reminder of home when fueled with all the strangeness of the outside world.

Your toddler will expect celebration from your trip out of your home. He or she will expect carousels and animals and special treats. Your child will want to run wild in a park, be that an amusement or simple, woodsy park. He or she will expect to spend quality time with you; and he or she will expect not to spend too much time away. All the excitement will become too much for them after several days.

To summarize:

Toddlers are assertive young adults. Pay heed. Talk to them about traveling. Prepare them. Excite them.

Be sure to keep zoos, safaris and/or parks on your itinerary.

Pack some snacks from back home, for when your toddler feels overwhelmed with unknown territory.

The Excited Children of the World: Seven Through Twelve-Year Olds

This is the peak age for family vacations. Seven through twelve-year-old children are older than their toddler counterparts; they reach for knowledge with zeal and they look forward to the new, strange sensory overload that is a vacation. Lucky for you, if you plan correctly, you can sort of marry your ideas of a parent vacation with a kid vacation. Given the correct, exciting information, your child will yearn to learn everything there is to know about an education cum beach-fun cum historical vacation.

But it's best to understand that your child can only take so much of one thing. If you have one day bursting with museums and education, try to counter it with another day of amusement park rides and/or strolling, running and boating around in a park. This way, you can have a layered vacation. You may find that you like the amusement park rides more than you know.

This is the very beginning of your child's conscious traveling. Therefore, you should allow them to be part of the packing. Give them a list of everything they'll need; be sure to double up on things like underwear and socks. Allow them to pack their bag; remind them specifically the best ways to do this with regards to their suitcase. This way, they'll feel responsible for their journey, and they'll understand the various important mechanisms behind the joy and adventure of a vacation.

Remember to continue to do similar things you would do with a small child while on vacation with your older child. Talk them through the strange things you're doing; allow them to understand exactly what happens in airport security and why, for example. You can tell them a bit more now that they're older. They might become fearful and confused when they're left in the dark about certain things. And remember to always have a few snacks on your person; how many

tantrums have you gotten out of in the past with just a spare cheese stick on hand?

To summarize:

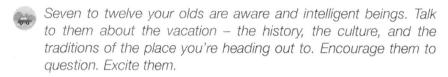

Seven to twelve your olds are aware and intelligent beings. Talk to them about the vacation – the history, the culture, and the traditions of the place you're heading out to. Encourage them to question. Excite them.

Give them a packing list. Ask them for their input. Then encourage them to pack their bags.

Talk to them about airport security and why things are the way they are. For their own safety. Education and experience go hand in hand.

Pack their favorite snacks for when food might become an issue.

Teenagers and Traveling

Your teenager is well on his or her way to become an opinionated adult. And this is why it's best to understand precisely what your specific teenager wants in a vacation. Keep your ways of communication incredibly open. Remember that your teenager can be moody and unresponsive. Allow him or her to open up and reveal their true expectations from their family vacation.

Once on the trot, be sure to give your teenager a bit of space in order to keep the peace. Your teenager might want to explore on his or her own; your teenager won't always want to be answerable to you. Allow them a brief vacation from a vacation. Perhaps, allow them to see a movie or a play on their own, and most definitely, give them some pocket money to spend as they like. Nothing like teen spirit and the fresh odor of independence. Let your teenager grow.

To summarize:

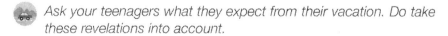

Ask your teenagers what they expect from their vacation. Do take these revelations into account.

Give your teenagers some pocket money and some independence while on vacation.

 Give them small chores. This will teach them responsibility.

Your Expectations: A Search for Adventure, Relaxation, and Your Inner Self

And finally, to your expectations. You desire a release from your day-to-day stress of work and family. But you must, of course, bring the family you've cultivated and brought to life along with you. This is both a blessing and a curse. Your past vacation plans may have seen you every day in a beach chair, soaking in the sun off the ocean. But your children will get hot and impatient, and they aren't allowed to sip on the sweet margaritas at the bar. Other vacations may have seen you at every imaginable museum in the area; but your toddler will tug at your clothes, demanding a snack and a nap.

With the proper techniques and planning, you can have the best of both worlds. You can show your children precisely what it is that you cherish so much about your chosen destination, and you can fuel yourself with the enthralling fun of a child's vacation. Someday, after all the family fun times have faded, you can recede back to your everyday beach chair vacation.

Chapter 3

A Focused Questionnaire
to Rectify Your Destination Dilemmas

Look to this family-friendly quiz to guide you to this year's proper family vacation destination. With all the children's needs and desires and your own stressors in mind, it's difficult to nail down the correct destination for your family's next vacation. However, asking yourself a series of questions and answering them honestly with regards to your family is one of the best manners in which to bring yourself to the sheer joy of several days out of town. After all, choosing the destination is just the beginning: the real fun lies in the learning and planning, both outlined in further chapters.

The truth is, whichever age bracket your children fall into, you can assimilate your vacation to fit their needs. Therefore, it's best to understand how best to suit your vacation to your specific family's personality based on the various things you like to do and the ways in which you like to do them. Answering the following questions honestly will ensure that your family has the best possible vacation.

Question 1: How many hours of outdoor activity would you say your family engages in on a weekly basis? This can include hiking, running, biking, or playing any sort of sport.

A. Zero to Three Hours.

B. Four to Seven Hours.

C. Seven or More Hours.

Question 2: How high would you describe you and your family's ability to try new, strange foods? For example: do you stick to your macaroni and cheese Mondays or do you branch out and try the new Chinese place down the street?

A. Low Ability

B. Medium Ability

C. High Ability

Question 3: Is your vacation pegged with a strict budget? Are you counting pennies to get your family out of the house?

A. Yes.

B. Only slightly. Everyone is on a budget, aren't they?

C. The sky is the limit.

Question 4: What sort of temperament is your family keen on for your vacation? Are you interested in warmth, for example, or are you uninterested in varied climates?

A. We search for dry, beach weather: anything for a relaxing day outdoors.

B. We don't mind the temperament so much; as long as it doesn't rain too much.

C. The climate doesn't matter; whatever happens can happen.

Question 5: How is your family's restaurant re quietly in a nice, ritzy restaurant? Or is fast food a must?

A. Fast food. Drive-thru. Anything but sitting down in public.

B. We can do large restaurants with other chaotic families. As long as we aren't the center of attention, we're good.

C. We can sit anywhere quietly; the children are incredibly composed.

Question 6: How familiar are you, the parent, with vacation planning? This may be your first vacation planning experience, for example, or it could be one of many: you understand the basics of itinerary planning and hotel selection and finding the best flights.

A. We're beginners; family vacation planning is a foreign language.

B. We understand the basics of transportation and hotel selection from out of town family events; however, we're in the dark about several vacation planning steps.

C. We've done it all before: we studied abroad, traveled after college, or worked around the world. We're hoping to gain insight on planning vacations with specific groups of children.

Question 7: What would you say is your level of ability to be spontaneous on vacation? For example, do you or one of your children suffer from any sort of plight that could sway your entire vacation if an episode erupts? Your child, for example, has asthma, and you've forgotten his inhaler. This sort of pre-planning forces you out of spontaneity into action-mode at all times; you must always be "on the lookout" for dangerous attacks.

A. Slim to none. Someone in our family suffers from something that keeps us on constant alert. We shouldn't be too far from familiar surroundings—be that our own city or a very close hotel room.

B. Our family's safety relies on structure; however, this does not sway us from occasional spontaneity. It's important, of course, to remain in public, close to authority figures who speak our own language.

C. We have no diseases or inhibiting factors: let our spontaneity roar. We can oam the world, camp for days, and fear not about forgetting any medicinal remedy. We are not tied down to our manmade products.

Question 8: How important would you say culture and education are for your desired vacation?

A. We're simply looking for a break; we don't need to talk to interesting people or broaden our minds. We just want to feel relaxed. Finally.

B. We're not opposed to new cultures or new ideas, but we're also interested in just buckets of fun and activity. A marriage of excitement and knowledge could be a nice suit.

C. We're interested in cramming as many museums and cultural events into our vacation as possible. We're looking to learn new languages, learn new cultures, learn everything.

Question 9: Do you have a transportation preference with regards to yourself or your children?

A. We prefer car, especially with baby and loud children incapable of long flights.

B. We have no preference; our children are capable of the quick travel found in flying, but the convenience and cost-friendly position of vehicle travel is alluring.

C. We prefer flying; we understand the implications of flying with children, and we accept them.

Question 10: How many days does your vacation allow?

A. 2-4 days.

B. 4-6 days.

C. More than 6 days.

Chapter 4

Analyzing Your Family Vacation Quiz Results

If you answered mostly A's...

...your family is not exactly fueled with the desire to branch out, try new, exciting things. And that's okay. It's still perfectly acceptable to need a break from your everyday schedule: and that, when you get down to it, is precisely what a vacation is. You and your children are no longer slaves to schedule. You are free to be a family together, to make up your own rules in whatever destination you decide.

Suggestion 1: Staycation

How much do you know about your own city, really? With flight and gas prices skyrocketing, many families have decided to stay in their own hometowns, exploring nearby areas they've never explored before, turning their own hometown into an undiscovered land. Your desire to break free from your every day schedule may lead you simply down the street.

It's best, however, to continue to treat your week break—your family's staycation—like a real vacation. Since you'll be staying either in your own bed or a hotel down the road, you'll have easy access to your normal routine. Do everything you would do to refute your normal life before leaving on an actual, out-of-town vacation. Finish your laundry and the rest of your chores before the actual beginning of your staycation. Don't even think about dropping by the office, even if it's right there and they need you. Think of yourself and your family as five hundred miles away from your real responsibilities and indulge yourselves. You won't be spending as much money by staying and vacationing in your hometown; but it's best to understand that you can spend a little bit more than usual. If you would usually go out to eat on vacation five hundred miles away, go ahead and treat yourself. (Be sure to go to a kid-friendly restaurant if your children are unable to handle fancy dining. Maybe you can get a babysitter at a later date for any of the more ritzy places.)

Furthermore, you cannot become lazy when planning your staycation. Be sure to pay attention to later chapters in this book to understand the ways in which to plan an itinerary. Of course, you do not always have to stick to your vacation itinerary. But at least having one on your staycation prevents you from slipping into bad habits like doing chores and watching too much television. This vacation is an attempt to rip you from your every day schedule. Allow it to do just that!

Website Research: Search for your own city's visitor website to understand better what attracts tourists to your city. Understand the role your particular town plays in the scheme of the world. Furthermore, look to www.yelp.com or tripadvisor.com for various reviews on local restaurants or hotels or fun businesses in your area that you've never tried before. This will leave a sense for various price ranges surrounding you.

Suggestion 2: Beach Vacation

Beach vacations are nice for the inactive families. The sandy beaches offer great expanses for your children to play in the sand, to read in the shade of an umbrella, or to run—if they so choose. Oftentimes, beach vacations allow for rented condos or great, beachside houses. While occasionally pricey, these beachside houses allow for much room for your family to spread out for a relaxing time away from your schedules. The beach houses come with several amenities as well such as cable television and video games if your children are more inclined to vacation couch side before joining you in the sun later on. The beach vacation is incredibly calm, oftentimes resort-like. Family-friendly restaurants lurk in all areas of beach life: restaurants full with loud, running children. Therefore, if you're searching for a low-key, unobtrusive place to take your entire family for an exciting dinner

away from it all, you should have several options.

Website Research: www.travel.usnews.com contains an elaborate list of best family beachside vacations. Further vacation homes can be found at www.homeaway.com.

If you answered mostly B's...

...your family holds within itself an innate curiosity. It isn't quite ready to break free from the country, for example. But it's interested in some sort of magic beyond the walls in which you live and breathe every day. Therefore, something familiar but also far away is essential. Your children will feel alive, fueled with the fact that they've heard a great deal about your destination but never thought they would arrive there. And you will feel excellent yielding this world to them: this world they've dreamed about.

A Local Theme Park, Disney World, or Orlando Studios: Search for Magic in a Pre-Ordained Family-Friendly Park

Theme parks throughout the world provide immense world building; therefore, no matter the age of your children, you should be able to find an elaborate park fresh with both young children rides and large rollercoasters for the most daring teenagers. Of course, it'll take a good deal of planning to understand which theme park is best for your particular family's personality. Cedar Point, for example, located in Northeastern Ohio, is generally perfect for a rollercoaster, thrill-seeking family while Disney World in Orlando, Florida is perfect for younger children, fresh and ready for the available Disney magic. Further younger-oriented families will find joy with Story Land, located in Glen, New Hampshire. It's based on German fairytale and is geared toward under-ten magic seekers.

Unfortunately, there are several other issues involved in planning a theme park vacation. Hotels surrounding Disney World, for example, are incredibly expensive. Luckily, you can do a bit of research in order to find various ticket and room deals, thus decreasing your overall vacation bill.

Website Research: www.disneyparks.disney.go.com lends you several tips on planning an extensive family vacation at Disney World. www.familyvacationcritic.com also outlines various ways in which theme park vacations can be beneficial for the entire family.

If you answered mostly C's...

...your family is aching to find a completely different world, to explore a completely different terrain.

Suggestion 1: A Large, European City

If money is no limit and your children are aching to explore another area of the world, you may find yourself in a strange, European city hobbling over cobblestone streets. When preparing for your European city vacation, however, remember maintain your children's needs as top priority. Try to position your hotel near a park; active children will need plenty of room to run freely in the otherwise great, somewhat strange city. Also, remember that it's best to stay in an area close to many of the main attractions. Travel is hard on children, and they will be unable to walk great distances. Try to continuously explain the historical significance of the city to your children while also lending them several children-friendly activities such as various local theme parks, park puppet shows, or pony rides.

Website Research: www.fodors.com outlines some of the best European cities for families. It includes Stratford-Upon-Avon and the

Italian coastal city of Cinque Terre.

Suggestion 2: A Camping Adventure

Bringing children into the wilderness without plumbing or local grocery stores seems like a crazy thing, sure. **But your family is adventurous and daring. Furthermore, reclining next to a campfire allows your children to really take charge in various situations.** They are able, for example, to perhaps prepare their own food over the fire, exchange stories, really commune about their lives at home. You are all so busy, living separate lives even as a family at home, it might be a good time to come together in this most ancient of communication arenas.

Furthermore, the location of your campground leaves a lot to be decided in additional planning. If you campground is close to a beach, for example, you can combine rugged adventure with a day of relaxation. Alternately, you can combine your rugged adventure with an even more rugged windsurfing expedition. There will be several local hiking trails, as well; most campgrounds contain various levels of difficulty, ranked from one to five, in order to administer to young children. Furthermore, several campgrounds contain kid-friendly horse rides. There's no end to the adventure your family can have out in the wilderness. Don't forget the s'more supplies.

Website Research: www.theguardian.com researches the ten greatest family camping spots in the world.

Discussing your destinations with other parents who've been to the same with their children will help give you an awesome kickstart with the pre-trip preparations. Log on to The Flying Kids website at www.theflyingkids.com for some real-time discussions.

Chapter 5

The Real Decision-Making Zone: Pre-Trip Preparations

Avoid Pitfalls Along the Way: Learn About Your Destination Before Departure

The hard part is over: you've chosen your destination. Safe in the confines of your living room, you and your children have discussed the pros and cons of various places discussed in Chapter 3. You've understood each other's vacation needs and are ready to dive head first into whatever vacation: be it halfway around the world or a quarter mile down the street.

However, the most important stage of any vacation lies in the planning and preparation. Without proper preparation, your vacation is a bit floppy and unstable. You're traveling or you're staycationing: either way, you're setting aside a time in your life to make beautiful memories with your children.

Culture Shock and Children: Discussing Culture Norms Beforehand Is Pivotal

You have bitter memories of times in your child's life; times when your child was anxious, unsure of his or her surroundings and unable to push through the haze of anger and tears. You understood, for example, that although the doctor's office was lit strangely, that although your child was interacting with a human he or she had never interacted with beforehand, that everything was fine. You understood that your doctor was administering proper shots for your child's health and safety. But your child had no real way of understanding that. Suddenly, their environment had changed, and you were unable to translate why.

Of course, in relation to this shot example, you got better at telling them exactly what to expect from the experience. This is precisely what you must do in order to eliminate any anxious feelings your child could feel in your new, vacation environment. You don't want your child's vacation—or your vacation—to be interrupted by this sheer confusion and anxious feeling. You want smooth sailing.

Essentially, culture shock is caused by the fact that a separate area of the world is mandated by different ideas, different ways of life. Therefore, the ways in which you've raised your own child— the things you've instilled in him or her—could differ with the ways in which your destination handles life events. Culture, however, is not limited to personal feeling. It also includes the food a people eat, the way they speak, and the way they behave socially. Depending on where you're going, everything could be different. Therefore, your child has understood one world: the world he/she calls home. It will be difficult for him or her to imagine that another world exists beyond the boundaries you've set in place.

Of course, going on vacation is all about removing those boundaries. It's all about allowing your children to understand that other cultures exist outside the tiny one they've come to understand. People speak different languages; the sun shines a little differently elsewhere. Yes— people eat snails in France. It's their culture. And because your child has had to understand that the momentary pain of the doctor's office shot is actually beneficial for his or her way of life, he or she can also understand that the world outside ought not to be feared, but to be appreciated for its diversity and beauty.

However, in order to allow your child maximum comfort while on vacation in a strange culture (or a strange hotel room down the street), you must continue a dialogue. You must tell them the various ways the place is different. The following sections outline specific details of the anti-culture shock plan.

Your Break from Cuisine Norms: Hot Dogs and Hamburgers

Staycation Cuisine Preparation

Your vacation decision has led you either to a hotel in your area or to rest, blissfully, in your own bedrooms. Flight prices and gas prices are ticking higher and higher, and who can blame you, really, for staying back and enjoying the scenery from where you stand?

That being said, a big part of any vacation lies in the cuisine. It's exciting, really, to embrace different restaurants throughout the world, from state to state and from country to country. Investigating another food culture is like the first step to investigating another world, to understanding the ways in which people live. For example: can you imagine using chopsticks for every meal, every day, your entire life?

When preparing for your Staycation, it's best to casually "run out" of the things normally lying around the house. That stuff lying around the house that you usually munch on is a part of your busy, work and

school culture. As vacationers, you are looking for variety and change.

Investigate the local cuisine scene. Are there any restaurants that emanate a culture that you haven't been to yet? Try looking on Yelp.com for any local restaurants with rave reviews. Go and try the restaurant with your family and leave a review yourself. In serving you, the vacationers, the restaurant owes you a solid, wonderful experience.

Furthermore, look to the safety of your own home to have a sort of "cuisine" departure. Grocery shop and splurge on "strange" items from around the world and administer a feast to your children that engages with the various ways people live outside of your town and country. For example, have a sushi night. Try out the curry recipes you've been dying to taste. Go ahead: have a taco night. Mexican food might be more conducive to sensitive child palates, anyway.

Resort and Amusement Park Cuisine Preparation

If your vacation plans include a great amusement park or resort, your cuisine plans are a little limited. However, taking a look at websites such as www.tripadvisor.com allows you to understand the various restaurants at these elaborate theme parks that are best for certain age groups. Disney World features an entire website devoted to descriptions and menus for their theme park restaurants. You already understand the foods your children like and appreciate—and these theme parks will be crawling with these foods: corndogs, fries, hot dogs, hamburgers, and pizzas. However, several of the theme park restaurants have sub-themes within themselves. Consider having a meal with an elaborately dressed cartoon character, for example, or drink milkshakes in an old convertible car in Magic Kingdom, emoting an age gone by: an age foreign and romantic to your children.

A theme park makes planning both easy and difficult. Its options for kid-friendly restaurants are expansive. Remember that part of the fun is engaging in a different sort of "culture." Prepare your children for something a little different than their average meal around the dinner table at home. Prepare them for magic!

Out-of-Country Cuisine Preparation

Out-of-Country Cuisine preparation obviously packs a heavy punch.

You don't want to leave your kids out to dry, picking at pieces of food that are both unfamiliar and unappetizing to them while people surrounding them at restaurants speak strange, foreign languages. That's a first class ticket to culture shock, absolutely.

Prior to arriving in the country you've chosen, you need to do a lot of research. If you have young children, you need to understand the kid-friendly restaurants versus the non-kid friendly restaurants. A Michelin-star chef, for example, will probably not serve a screaming toddler. (Check www.craigslist.com for available babysitters if you want one night alone with your spouse.) The world has McDonald's around every corner.

However, if you'd like to experience a different country's cuisine with your children, there are several ways to prepare them. If you are heading across waters to Paris, France, for example, prepare them for a typical French meal. Include the snails, if you're daring. Explain to them that the French people eat very differently from you. Tell them the various things usually found on the menu: foie gras, escargots, crepes, etc. And explain to them that in order to understand a culture, they should try the various things a culture promotes in its cuisine.

Furthermore, almost every big city has a to-go stand with the local cuisine. Istanbul promotes kebabs around every corner, while London passes out fish and chips by the second. A quick picnic in the park while experiencing the local cuisine might be just the thing for your thriving, culture-curious family.

Camping Cuisine Preparation

The camping cuisine offers a whole new spectrum for your preparation. As a family surrounding a campfire, you are all meant to prepare the meals outdoors. Like the original pioneers and forbearers to your area, you will defend your livelihood utilizing nature.

Familiarize your children with the foods you'll be cooking

over the fire and allow them to understand that, perhaps for the first time ever, they are responsible for their own dinner. They must deposit their stick containing a hot dog, whatever, over the fire safely and responsibly. This is their livelihood for the evening.

Furthermore, remember that since you're on vacation in a place where you might not be driving or trotting away from mother nature, it's best to pack several coolers full of snacks and supplies. Ask your children their opinions of the various snacks they'd like out in the wilderness. They're going on vacation with you; they're going to be swimming and hiking and playing and sleeping on the ground. Allow them to choose a few snacks of their own. Amazingly, sleeping outside, without the safety of a roof and television, can really take your children out of their comfort zone, out of their culture. Allow them to keep a few familiar items.

To summarize:

 The food you will eat on vacation will be a part of the culture shock you might receive. Prepare your kids. Tell them about the oddities of the cuisine they will be experiencing.

 Encourage kids to come out of their comfort zone to try something new, so as to blend into the culture.

 If camping, do keep some snacks as emergency food.

Weather Investigation

Remember: when preparing your packing list, you must consider that your destination may – and chances are that it will - have a different climate. You must pack accordingly so as not to be stuck abroad without your proper winter coat, for example. You want your children to remain as cosy as possible at all times in their new environment; dress them comfortably.

If you need to pack for cold weather, remember to pack layers. Anything that imbibes dampness should not be close to the skin. If you are planning on being out in the weather quite often, sightseeing, it's best to wear tight, dry things close to yours skin. If your children are damp throughout the day, they'll be grumpy, cold, and wet. That is a ripe equation for illness. And illness on vacation is an absolute tragedy.

Furthermore, if you're planning on driving to your vacation destination, it's best to understand the weather forecast prior to your departure. Be certain that your tires have proper traction in case the roads become slick; be sure that you have the proper tools to repair any damaged tire, any dead battery, at any time of the day, as well.

To Summarize:

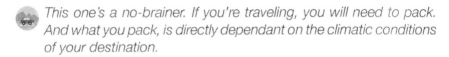 *This one's a no-brainer. If you're traveling, you will need to pack. And what you pack, is directly dependant on the climatic conditions of your destination.*

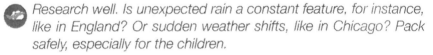 *Research well. Is unexpected rain a constant feature, for instance, like in England? Or sudden weather shifts, like in Chicago? Pack safely, especially for the children.*

If you'll be driving, be sure to check weather forecasts everyday.

Understand Your Surroundings' Safety Options

No one wants to consider it: but one aspect of your vacation planning must include the possibility of disaster. Therefore, it's best to familiarize yourself with the ways you can protect or report any disasters. No matter where you are, life can take a hold of you and change the course of everything.

If you're staying in your hometown, you obviously understand the emergency phone number and the hospital locations. Understand the plan of emergency at the theme park of your chosen destination, as well. For example, a quick research on the Disney World website tells that a swift 911 dial from anywhere in the park alerts Reedy Creek, Disney World's number one emergency provider. Anyone transported from Disney World Resorts to the hospital via ambulance is transported free of charge. Become familiar with the emergency protocol at your chosen amusement park.

If you're embarking to a different country, you must mark both the country code and the emergency phone number. For example,

France's emergency number is 112, and their country code is +33. Therefore, as an example, if you're utilizing your out of country cell phone, you'll have to press +33 (112) in order to contact the authority figure.

Furthermore, it's best to know where your country's embassy is in relation to where you're staying abroad. If something drastic happens, like if your passport is stolen, you'll want the backup your country's embassy can provide.

Your camping trip allows for several park-watchers; there will, for instance, always be a park ranger on duty at all time. Understand the place in the parks to journey for an emergency. And always have a first-aid kit for minor emergencies; after all, nature is something the modern man is not accustomed to, unfortunately.

To summarize:

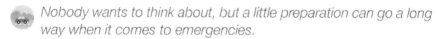 Nobody wants to think about, but a little preparation can go a long way when it comes to emergencies.

 Memorize the country and area codes of your destination(s).

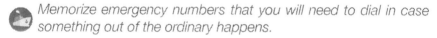 Memorize emergency numbers that you will need to dial in case something out of the ordinary happens.

 Be mindful of first aid procedures and help centers, when in the great outdoors.

Passport and Documents Preparations

Regardless of his or her age, your child must have a passport if you are leaving the country. Therefore, if you've decided you're traveling away from home, ready for greener pastures, you have quite a few steps to make a passport a reality.

A passport application for a minor must be submitted at your local passport agency or office. Look for the rules and requirements for a successful application.

Ensure that you yourselves have valid passports as well. If you haven't traveled in a while, give that expiration date a peak. Many countries require a passport valid for at least 3 or 6 months from the date of entry / visa approval. Make sure you're all set, and well in time. In most cases, expediting your passport's renewal will cost you a lot more, so it's crucial to begin the process at least six weeks ahead of your travel dates.

To Summarize:

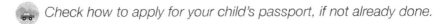 *Check how to apply for your child's passport, if not already done.*

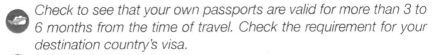 *Check to see that your own passports are valid for more than 3 to 6 months from the time of travel. Check the requirement for your destination country's visa.*

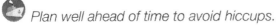 *Plan well ahead of time to avoid hiccups.*

Familiarize Yourself with the Local Language

If your travels take you far from the realms of your oh-so-breezy English language, the chances of your child's culture shock skyrocket. Therefore, it's beneficial to familiarize your children with the sounds of the language prior to arriving. You can make it a project and learn a few words every day. Learn simple, every day words like thank you, good morning, hello, etc. Try to learn the ways in which you order food in the new language, as well, so you can get along at a restaurant or in a shop.

Fortunately, smartphones and tablets today have created a wonderful concoction of options to choose from. There are several language learning applications that you can download to your phone or computer in order to not only expedite the learning process, but to make it fun as well.

Anki Language Application
Anki means "memorizing" in Japanese: and look, you're already learning. The

application is a free flashcard program. It lends you a word and image; it may play a sound to allow your brain to make a connection between the word, the image, and the

sound. Children are especially receptive to sounds and colors, making Anki a great possibility for enabling them to learn a few words and phrases.

Duolingo Language Application

Duolingo is free on for Android and iOS devices. It approaches language-learning in a unique manner. Essentially, on Duolingo, you're required to read things that actual speakers and writers of the language are writing on the Internet. It is kind of like the Wikipedia of language learning, if you may. Everybody's a teacher and everybody's a student. It also offers quite a few options for dictations and visualizations. Furthermore, it understands the things you struggle with along the way and adjusts your progress as you go. And what an interactive teacher it is!

The Pimsleur Method

This audio-based language learning application focuses on sound exercises. Any child familiar with kindergarten and rhyming would respond well to this application. There are several grammar exercises, but Pimsleur's focus is on hearing. This may be beneficial, in the long run, as you probably won't be doing a whole lot of reading other than English perhaps, on vacation. Listening to the people with whom you speak at restaurants and boutiques and on the street, however, will take up all your time, and you may thank Pimsleur more than your lucky stars for an enhanced, interactive experience.

To Summarize:

We can not stress enough, the importance of learning some of the foreign language you're about to encounter.

See above for some fun and useful Android and iOS apps.

Familiarize Yourself with your Transportation Options

Traveling to a separate culture pushes you far from the comforts of your family's minivan. Changing your mode of transportation can be a little alarming for your children and potentially contribute to anxiety and fear, especially if your transportation includes a lot of chaos and maneuvering.

A lot of this you cannot change; however, you can prepare yourself to embark upon these various transportation routes. If you appear sure of yourself, your children will sense this and feel calm. To be honest, transportation is one of the most exciting parts of any journey. Make sure you don't spoil the experience.

Staycation Transportation

If your staycation is taking you downtown, try leaving your minivan in the hotel parking lot and experiencing your city from a different perspective. You understand your city from the seat of your minivan. Pulling your family from those sticky seats and allowing them to appreciate the various mass transportations of the city will add a bit of sparkle to your staycation.

Inspect the travel options you have, allowing you to go from your hotel to the great monuments or attractions in your area. Your hotel may have a shuttle bus that runs from the hotel to various museums, as well. If your hotel is downtown, you can try walking a little bit to local restaurants. That's true immersion. It will feel nothing like the city you thought you knew.

Theme Park Transportation

If the hotel in which you've opted to stay is in any way connected to the theme park you've chosen as your destination, your transportation should be covered. Check shuttle bus times and don't worry about navigating the greater city—unless you'd like to explore. If you'd like your own vehicle, and you haven't brought your own, there are several car rental options. Check www.avis.com, www.enterprise.com or www.hertz.com.

Out-of-Country Transportation

Embarking out of the country lends an entirely new angle to transportation. You must somehow rally your children—after a long plane ride—along the proper path to your hotel room utilizing the local bus, metro or taxi. Then again, you must hit the mass transportation trail in order to cover the sights and sounds. It sounds like a nightmare, and it can be, if you don't prepare.

Research ahead of time to ensure you have the appropriate money to pay for your public transportation tickets. Many metro stations might not accept international credit or debit cards; thus, you must have the appropriate currency at hand. You can exchange money at the airport

prior to mounting the public transportation.

Always have snacks. Public transportation rides can be lengthy, especially if you're riding from the airport to the inner city. Do as you've always done before soccer matches, school events, or play dates: arm your child with his or her favorite snacks to keep him or her occupied and his glucose levels revving. If your child is alert and not grumpy with hunger, he or she will be much more receptive while on the train.

Download the appropriate phone applications to ensure you always have a local transportation map. Your chosen city will probably have

some public transportation applications of its own; here are a few well-rated, generic transportation applications:

Moovit: A Live Transit App Covering 120 Cities Worldwide

iPhone application Moovit utilizes modern technology in order to update you on arrival and departure times for you chosen city. You can understand alternate routes from place to place based on your schedule. The application gives you step-by-step directions and even directs your walking routes, to and from a transit point. The application uses enhanced technology: the more people that utilize Moovit, the more accurate the arrivals, departures and alerts are.

Metro: A World of Subway Maps

This application allows you to download and utilize metro maps from all over the world. Get from point A to point B easily with just a quick perusal on this free service. Give your children a sense that you know what you're doing with the excellent Metro facilities.

Taxi Magic: When Public Transportation Becomes Too Much For One Day

Perhaps your long day of traveling and city-exploring has put everyone in a grouchy, tired mood. Vacations can be exhausting. Therefore, if you're anxious to be back in the hotel room and you don't want to take another look at your Metro map, look to the free Taxi Magic application. You can make free online bookings, charge the taxi ride to your credit card, and track your arriving cab through updates.

Camping Transportation

If you're flying out towards your campsite, you may want to look into renting a vehicle at the arrival airport in order to facilitate carrying with you all the supplies you'll need on the campground. Firewood is a bit tricky to wield on the metro; and most metros don't take you out to the forest.

If you are looking to camp and rent a vehicle in a foreign country, you might need to apply for an International Driving Permit. Some countries will accept your local country's driving license. Check what's the case at your destination.

To Summarize:

 Transportation can be fun, if you're well prepared.

 See if you can cover the city by foot. It would be great for immersion into the local culture.

 If you will be using the metro or bus networks, make sure you have local currency for purchasing tickets and passes. Familiarize yourself with maps online or via any of the apps mentioned above.

 Renting a car? Make sure you'll be allowed to drive. Will they require an international driving permit or will your local license suffice?

Accommodation Arrangements

Staycation Accommodation

You probably know and understand the hotels in your hometown. However, a closer look at www.kidscantravel.com can give you a sense for the family-friendly hotels in your area. TripAdvisor.com is excellent to lend you insight on the actual sizes of hotel rooms and the actual services provided. You can't always trust the hotel website, but you can trust fellow vacationers to tell you if their money was utilized optimally.

Of course, if you're opting to stay home due to cost, your accommodation lies before you. Because hotels are usually a part of the vacation experience, try not to spend too much time at home. That can be a bummer.

Theme Park Accommodation

Every theme park around the world hosts its own character-laden resorts and hotels. Several theme parks provide family-friendly hotels, meal plans, and park tickets in an all-inclusive, easy-to-purchase package; find these packages on the relevant theme park's official website.

If you'll be visiting a themepark in the US, www.parkhotel.com allows you to search for hotels based on location. The website yields a list of all the popular theme parks, zoos, and waterparks across the country. Furthermore, your hotel can become your theme park. Several hotels become their own vacation getaways. For example, Fallsview Indoor Waterpark includes a massive indoor waterpark with sixteen waterslides. This indoor adventure is just a five minute walk from Niagara Falls, allowing this vacation to have two parts: theme park adventure and as well as the outdoors.

Out-of-Country Accommodation

Searching for kid friendly out-of-country accommodations can be tricky. Often times, families will opt for actual apartments in their vacation destination. This way, they have all the amenities of their home. For example, you can cook your child's favorite meal for lunch if you want to take a break from the wild, wild, wild world. You can have a home base for your children to feel free and unrestrained by the tight walls of many hotel rooms. Excellent options for finding apartments abroad can be found at www.HomeAway.com or www. Vacation-Apartments.com.

Budget families traveling abroad can opt for hostels. Although they sound a little scary, hostels are actually a completely valid way to vacation in great cities across the world like Barcelona, Athens, and many Asian countries like Bali or Tokyo. Hostels are clean and friendly, for backpackers, older people, and families. Gone are the days when

these played host to young nomads only. Several of the rooms have up to six beds, allowing your entire family to share a budget-friendly room. Furthermore, hostels usually come with a kitchen, allowing you to cook for your children without hassle. Hostels are sure to provide a creative spin on your vacation; each hostel has a unique character. Look to www.HostelWorld.com or www.HostelBookers.com for hostel reviews and costs.

Furthermore, staying out in the countryside can offer reasonably reduced accommodation cost. The small town of Fussen in Germany, for example, lends a spectacular view of Germany's mountains and lakes. Imagine making it base, and then, taking a day trip to nearby Munich if you crave city life. Imagine spending other days windsurfing, swimming and horseback riding in the country. If that's your cup of tea, then arrange your stays accordingly.

If you'd like to opt for a hotel room for your family, there are several ways to find excellent accommodation. Look to www.TravelandLeisure. com's yearly list of best family hotels throughout the world; you might find one in your vacation city. If you're opting out of the fabulous home base an apartment can provide, it's best to understand what your child requires in a hotel. Your child will want to feel like there's something a little special for them at the hotel you've chosen; several hotels offer kiddie goodie bags, kid-only game rooms, and kid-friendly activities like teddy bear tea parties. Your hotel should welcome your children like honored guests in order to allow them to feel safe, comfortable. It is also important to check to see if they will allow for extra bedding for older children in the room.

Make sure you're staying close to public transportation. Whether you're opting for an apartment or a hotel, you can not afford to be at an arduous walk from the first bus stop or metro station. This will especially be true when you're traveling with younger kids, and most importantly, with baby buggies or strollers or lots of backpacks. Staying close to public transportation gives the right kick to the start of your day. You step out of your hotel or apartment and alight the bus, the tram or the train within minutes. That's bliss!

Also make sure that if you'll be using buggies or strollers, both your hotel and nearby metro stations have friendly escalators and/or elevators.

Preparing Your Campsite Accommodation

Camping is unique in that most often, you arrive to the site carrying your accommodation in a bag or a box. If you don't have your own tent, the occasional campsite will offer tent rental. Be sure to research this beforehand.

However, preparing your campsite accommodation safely is incredibly important. Clear your campsite of any tree limb debris in order to maintain a safe environment for your children. Allow your children to assist in tent building. Align the tents in a circle, at least ten feet away from the designated campfire.

Set up different areas for different activities around your campsite. Your campsite should feel like a prepared vacation "home" to allow your children to feel safe and protected. Formulate a living room around the fire by setting out your lawn chairs. Maintain a food preparation table, provide a clearing for running and playing, and designate a kids' tent and an adult tent. Be sure to issue boundaries for clear, open camping communication.

To Summarize:

 The accommodation is the single, most important aspect of your vacation. Book yours with love and attention.

 Ask yourself: would your family be better suited for a hotel or an apartment?

 Make sure the hotel is kid-friendly: allowing for your kids in the room, perhaps have some special entertainment packages for children, has elevators, and is close to a metro with escalators or elevators to accommodate strollers.

 At theme parks, it is probably best to stay at a theme park resort or hotel. These will enable on-site fun for the children as well as free shuttles to and from the parks.

 Camping paraphernalia needs special care. Make sure you've ticked everything off the list. Set up a family-friendly campsite. For pointers, please read above.

Modes of Transportation to be Used

 Decide the mode of transportation you're going to take to get to your hotel or apartment BEFORE you arrive at the airport. If you opt for the train, for example, you should already understand where to go, how long the walk will take from baggage claim area, and where your train stop is in relation to your hotel. If a train does not arrive close enough to your hotel, you may need to opt for a taxi or a bus. A bus is most likely the most inconvenient option at this point; they're quite cramped and stop more often than the train, forcing you and your children in transit for a long, long time.

Granted, of course, that the bus is often your most budget friendly option, this isn't the best time to be penny-wise. The taxi, on the other hand, will be the most expensive albeit convenient option. A lifesaver, actually! So if your children are too cranky or feeling sick from all the traveling, this might be the time to dig a little deeper into your pockets. Try to agree on a set price with your taxi driver prior to departing from the airport, unless the city is served by metered taxis. In the European city of Paris, for example, a taxi ride from the airport to the center of Paris should set you back no more than fifty euros. This may be an appropriate price to pay with your humongous, family-sized luggage and overtired, edgy children.

 Also decide how you will be traveling at your destination. Read the following chapter 6 for more details on this.

Chapter 6

Planning: Developing your itinerary

Don't assume you can take to your vacation with all-day, everyday spontaneity. When you bring kids along, spontaneity isn't always an option. It's best to plan every day of your vacation in order to maximize your time, your energy, and your health. Keep in mind that the most important factor of your vacation is relaxation. A planned itinerary makes sure you have covered all bases.

Involve Kids in the Process

When planning your itinerary, be sure to include any older children and teenagers in the process. Ask your teenager to form a list of the absolute must-sees and must-dos. This will tell them that you respect them enough to make a few choices in your vacation. Your teenager isn't a child anymore; he or she is ripe with opinions.

You should make a list of the things you'd like to see as well. Generally, younger children are along for the ride; however, it's up to you and your teenager to be responsible for that ride. It's up to you to make it comfortable for them.

We recommend it would be a good idea for you to give them a fun assignment. Tell them what you'd like on your vacation, and ask them to come up with an itinerary that encompasses yours and their expectations. They should be encouraged to research attractions, restaurants, shops and theatre. Then discuss. Revise. Discuss. Revise. Next, make a list of all the things your younger children enjoy doing. Ask your teenager's input on this. Allow them to understand that a sufficient amount of park play, swimming, and hiking will complete up your vacation. Happy young children mean a happy you.

To Summarize:

 Your vacation is now just around the corner. Start preparing your itinerary.

 Include your children in the process. Make it fun. Tell them what you want to see. Ask them to research and say what they'd like to do on vacation. Encourage them to come up with an itinerary. Discuss. Revise. Discuss. Revise. Finalize.

Weather and Travel Considerations

Next, consider weather and travel issues. For example, if you'd like your itinerary to include outdoor activities, you must be prepared for any pitfalls. Rain can be unpredictable, and therefore, you must work quickly to switch activities throughout the week. Always have a backup plan. A rained out park afternoon on Monday, for example, can be swapped with a museum afternoon on Wednesday. However, if your children require run around playtime, you may need to search for an indoor, interactive activity. Have several indoor and outdoor activities on the docket to meet everyone's needs.

Furthermore, after a full day of traveling to your destination, your children might not be ready to dive into the action-packed sequence of events you may want your first day to contain. Don't push your children too hard; even the best children can become confused and agitated in new environments, especially if they're tired. It's best to ease them into it.

To Summarize:

 While preparing your itinerary, keep in mind weather conditions.

 In order to be prepared for unexpected rain on an outdoorsy day, either swap another day's activities with the drenched day or keep a fall back plan/itinerary for such days.

 Do not over tire the kids. Keep in mind stamina.

Peruse the Local Map

When you're planning each day's itinerary, take a look at a local map. You won't want to travel too much of a distance each day, and you'll want to keep the public transportation to an all-out minimum. For example, if you're dying to see a specific museum on Tuesday, inspect the map to see if there are any kid-friendly parks and other must-visit attractions in the area. Take a look online to understand the food options in that area, as well. Circle the area in which you'll spend that day; understand the public transportation route you'll have to take to get there, and stay there. Most cities are planned into sections. For example, spending a day in Paris' Marais lends you a look at Notre Dame, the Musée de la Magie (the magic museum), the Centre Pompidou, many park and take away food options. You don't have to leave the area until you retreat back to your accommodation, ready to rest up for another day. In order to stay organized, try making color coordinated routes for each day. Tuesday, for example, is blue. Circle the routes and any metro stop changes you'll have to make on your way to Tuesday's destination with a blue marker.

To Summarize:

 Use the local city and metro maps for your destination while preparing your itinerary.

Try to master the city, by conquering one area at a time. Mark all attractions in each area and try and fit them them all into a day each. One area at a time. This should keep traveling time to a minimum.

 Colour code your days and routes.

Day-by-Day Travel Itinerary: Keep It Simple

When you begin your day-by-day travel itinerary, you must, in the end, base it on your youngest child. Your youngest child can handle the least and will get tired the quickest. Therefore, if you don't feel your youngest child can handle too much, choose one thing from either your (or your teenager's) extensive list of must-do items for each day. Just one item will not overwhelm any young children, and it sets your expectations safely low. Fill the rest of your itinerary with activities or sightseeing that your young child will like or at the very least, be most easily managed at. Good examples are picnics in the park, horseback rides, hiking or swimming. If your child is feeling a little bit energetic on a particular day, you can add more things from the designated list of must-do things. Therefore, you can have a set item for each day in a designated area; the rest of the day allows for continued exploration of that area doing the various things your child enjoys. This low-level stress itinerary keeps things simple. It keeps everyone happy.

Our Parents' Travel Guide allows for intelligent and sensitive planning for families. There are many destination specific guides to help parents plan the perfect itinerary, keeping in mind, all of the pointers covered so far. It would be worthwhile to check if your destination is covered in this series. Each guide carries a sample itinerary along with helpful routes for each day.

A recommended template is produced below for your benefit.

To Summarize:

 When all is said and done, your itinerary needs to give the most leeway to the youngest member of the family.

 Try to be somewhat flexible to his/her moods and needs. Plan to accomplish some of your and the older kids' expectations. And leave the remaining time to be utilized according to the youngest

one's energy level and needs.

 Our Parents' Travel Guide Series covers most of the major destinations of the world. Check to see if we've covered your destination. These guides come with planned itineraries and routes.

Template: Sample Itinerary for a Family's Day Out in Paris. Appendix 1 (at the end of this book) has a blank templates for you to print out and fill in for your own vacation.

Day 1 · Arc de Triomphe — Champs-Elysées — Place de Concorde — Jardin de Tuileries

Schedule	Destination/ attraction	How to get there	Need to take into account	Comments
9:30-12:00	Arc de Triomphe	métro stop Charles de Gaulle-Etoile. metro line 2, 6, or 1	travel to the top hours: 10:00-23:00, last entry at 22:15	Buy tickets at the base. Adults €9.50. Children under 18 are free.
12:00-14:00	Walking in the Champs-Elysées	Stroll from the Arc de Triomphe down the refined shopping of the Champs-Elysées	Not to miss: Mercedes-Benz store	shops and cafés are usually quite expensive
14:00-14:45	Place de la Concorde	Place de la Concorde is at the end of the Champs-Elysées	This square is always open	Tell the kids: The Obelisk of Luxor is 72 feet tall, weighing 220 tons!.
14:45 – 17:00	Jardin des Tuileries	Walking from Place de la Concord	The park is open to the public before sundown. Kids activities tend to happen on Wednesdays, Saturdays, and Sundays	Ferris Wheel prices: €10 for adults; €5 for children under 10

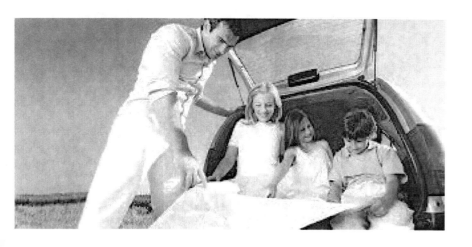

Provide Incentive for Children's Best Behavior

Tell your children that if they remain on their best behavior while doing that one thing that you've chosen for the day (a museum or church, for example), they will receive a treat. This can range from a small ice cream or an entire afternoon at the city's zoo. Keep things fun, light and positive. Do not threaten your children by taking away things they want to do on the itinerary. Your child is alarmed at the strangeness of their environment, and may be acting outside of his or her normal personality.

To Summarize:

 Children may be difficult at times during travel. Do not punish them, but introduce a reward program for good behaviour.

Chapter 7

The Packing Checklist

We cannot stress enough the importance of carrying luggage with wheels. There are several kinds - the ones that roll smoothly in only one direction at about a 45 degree incline, and the ones with 360 degree rolling wheels. Get the kind you are most comfortable with, and give them a test drive, just to ensure good quality. Make sure you are comfortable using one hand pulling the luggage easily while holding your kids in your other hand, if that is to be the scenario. You need friendly luggage to steer you on footpaths, and in out of trains and buses. Never choose suitcases without wheels. Better to be swift on the move than to strain your arms unnecessarily.

Also, if you're thinking of investing in new bags for the trip, do check the lightweight varieties on offer these days. True, they are a tad

expensive, but the combination of sturdy and weightless is a valuable combination you will agree. Luggage is a long-term investment. Make your decision wisely.

In addition to suitcases, you are also advised to get your children a backpack each. The ones that are both light and rainproof will be your best bet. These will come in handy on the flight, during car and train travel, and while on the trot each day.

Involve Kids in the Process when planning your itinerary, be sure to include any older children and teenagers in the process. Ask your teenager to form a list of the absolute must-sees and must-dos. This will tell them that you respect them enough to make a few choices in your vacation. Your teenager isn't a child anymore; he or she is ripe with opinions. You should make a list of the things you'd like to see as well. Generally, younger children are along for the ride; however, it's up to you and your teenager to be responsible for that ride. It's up to you to make it comfortable for them.

For the Flight

☑ A book to read

☑ An activity book

☑ Some pencils

☑ Some light snacks

☑ Video games, an mp3 player or a tablet that your child might plan to carry

☑ Some chewables for take-off and landing

☑ Sanitary wipes

☑ Our Kids' Travel Guide Series. There may one specifically for your destination!

For Longer Journeys on the Car, Train or Bus

☑ A book to read

☑ An activity book

☑ Some pencils

☑ Some light snacks

☑ Electronic mobile devices your child might plan to carry

☑ Sanitary wipes or anti-bacterial lotion

☑ A bottle or thermos of water or juice

☑ Anti-nausea over-the-counter chewable medication

☑ Our Kids' Travel Guide Series. There may one specifically for your destination!

For Days Out

☑ Some light snacks

☑ Sanitary wipes or anti-bacterial lotion

☑ A bottle or thermos of water or juice

☑ Anti-nausea over-the-counter chewable medication

☑ A cap

☑ A disposable raincoat

☑ Sunglasses

☑ Sandals for the beach

☑ A ball and/or a frisbee for the park

☑ Sunscreen lotion

Now, for your packing list for the suitcases.

Baby's First Packing Checklist
Your tiny baby needs quite a bit of stuff for your travels.

☑ Diapers: one diaper for every hour you'll be traveling to your destination

☑ 5 diapers per day

☑ Changing Pad for Diaper Changes

☑ Blankets for Travel

☑ Plastic Bags for Soiled Diapers

☑ Diaper Rash Cream

☑ Wipes

☑ Airplane-safe disinfectant hand gel

☑ Extra pacifiers

☑ Toys for your baby

☑ Clothes, socks, shoes: two outfits per day

☑ Bathing suit

☑ Washable bibs

☑ Sun hat (depending on weather)

☑ Formula

☑ Extra bottles and nipples

☑ Nightlight for evening diaper changes

☑ First-aid kit

☑ Baby sling for carrying your baby around your destination

☑ Portable crib for your accommodation

☑ Collapsible stroller for easy transport through cities and theme parks

☑ Phone number of baby's doctor in order to contact him or her with any aliments

Toddler Packing List

Your toddler's packing list is similar to the one above, especially if they're still wearing diapers for the long trip.

- ☑ Diapers (if applicable): 5 per day.

- ☑ Changing Pad for Diaper Changes

- ☑ Blankets for Travel

- ☑ Plastic Bags for Soiled Diapers

- ☑ Diaper Rash Cream

- ☑ Wipes

- ☑ Airplane-safe disinfectant hand gel

- ☑ Toys and books

- ☑ Easy snack foods

- ☑ Clothes, socks, shoes: two outfits per day.

- ☑ Bathing suit

- ☑ Sun hat

- ☑ Nightlight

- ☑ First-aid kit

- ☑ Collapsible stroller for easy transport through cities and theme parks

- ☑ Phone number of toddler's doctor in order to contact him or her with any ailments

Kid's Packing List

Your child may not be ready to pack for himself, but allow him to have some say in the t-shirts and toys he'd like to bring on your vacation. Allow him to feel included, but also monitor everything that enters his suitcase.

- ☑ 1 outfit per day

☑ 2 extra shirts for emergency

☑ 1 extra pair of pants

☑ 1 dress-up outfit for nice restaurants (if applicable)

☑ sweatshirts and sweaters (if weather calls for it)

☑ windbreaker (if applicable)

☑ walking shoes

☑ socks and underwear for each day with two extra pairs each

☑ 2 swimsuits

☑ familiar snacks/familiar food items

☑ toys, books, games, etc.

Packing List for You and Your Teenage Child

Allow your teenager to pack for him or herself. However, be sure to pass along this extensive packing list. Furthermore, you, the adult, should be in charge of your children's toiletry items and first aid items.

☑ One outfit per day

☑ 2 extra shirts

☑ 1 extra pair of pants

☑ 1 or 2 formal outfits

☑ Pajamas

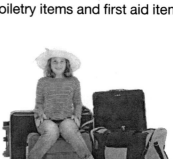

☑ Exercise/outdoor outfit

☑ Underwear and socks with two extra pairs each

☑ Rain jacket/windbreaker

☑ Walking shoes

☑ Formal walking shoes

☑ Sun hat

☑ Shampoo (for entire family)

☑ Conditioner (for entire family)

☑ Any hair products/accessories

☑ Soap

☑ Deodorant

☑ Toothbrushes (for entire family)

☑ Toothpaste

☑ Beach towels (if not included with hotel)

☑ Aspirin or Advil

☑ Motion sickness medicine

☑ Band-Aids

☑ Hand sanitizer

☑ Prescription medication

☑ Sunscreen

☑ Insect repellant

☑ Credit cards

☑ Health insurance information

☑ Passports

☑ International Driver's Permit (if applicable)

☑ Tickets or Confirmations for various events

☑ Photocopies of your important documents

☑ Sunglasses

☑ Cell phone and charger

☑ Money belt

☑ Camera and camera charger

☑ Electrical adapter/converter

To Summarize:

 Invest in good, lightweight luggage that comes with wheels. Give them a test drive beforehand.

 Get featherweight, rainproof backpacks for the kids.

 See the above for detailed checklists on what to pack.

For more insights and tips from fellow parent travelers, click through to our online resources at www.theflyingkids.com. Log on for useful advice, ratings, do's and don't, how-to's by other parents who have been there, done that. And of course, your own insight, questions, and comments will add to the plethora of resources at FlyingKids. We're all about traveling families.

Chapter 8

Planning
Your Vacation Budget

Our Vacation Budget

Scrimping and saving for your family vacation can be both exciting and exhausting. You want your vacation to live up to your expectations, but you don't want to break the bank in the process. Therefore, no matter where you've decided to vacation this year: whether you're heading to your city's downtown, across the country, or across the world, it's best to prepare a vacation budget and stick to it. That way, when you arrive home, you'll have no extenuating bills to cloud your fabulous vacation memories.

Vacation Spending - The Three Areas

The three areas of vacation spending are transportation, accommodation, and, of course, fun. Transportation costs can include your flight tickets, your transportation to and from the airport, and any transportation you must utilize while in your destination of choice. Accommodation costs are for your hotel, apartment, hostel, or campground of choice. Dining cost must be ascertained. And entertainment costs include everything in between: the food you buy at the airport, for example, or the museum or cinema tickets you purchase for a day in the middle of your vacation.

Make accommodation and travel arrangements based on your budget, and not vice versa. So if it's incredibly expensive to travel to your desired location, do not splurge on your accommodation. Stay in the cheapest hostel or hotel you can find in order to enjoy all the things a city has to offer. Furthermore, if you're having a staycation, your transportation costs are incredibly low. Therefore, you can splurge a little bit in other areas like restaurants, activities, or hotel accommodations. If you're on a tight budget, compromise on one area of spending for a little spoiling and TLC in the other.

Set Yourself a Daily Spending Allowance

There's no better time to limit yourself to cash spending than when you're on vacation. Set yourself a cash limit each day in a specified envelope. When the envelope is empty for the day, you're simply done spending money. Of course, you can utilize your credit card for emergencies and spontaneous decisions. But if you want to maintain a strict budget while maintaining a good level of fun, spending an allotted amount each day is the way to go.

Consider giving your children a daily or weekly spending allowance. Take from the budget you've laid out for your entire family, and give each child (if they're old and responsible enough) an allotted amount of money to spend as he or she pleases throughout the week. That means they can spend it all in one place on the first day—and miss out on something they really want at the end of the week. This is a great way to demonstrate the importance of budgeting your money.

Alternately, you can decide to give them some money to spend every day. They can either spend it all, save it for something towards the end, or spend some and save some along the way. Allow them to manage their money.

Understand Any Out-of-Country Cost Conversions

When traveling out of the country, you should understand the conversion rate, and whether that works to your advantage or not. Make sure at the time of developing your budget, that you're outlining expenses and disposable cash in the local currency of your destination. This will help keep things in perspective.

Watch Out for Hidden Fees

Be sure you understand precisely what is included in your hotel/hostel accommodations. If the parking is not included and you've chosen to drive to the accommodation, for example, you could rack up an extra fifty dollars a day. Utilize everything free at your hotel, like the pool, as well. If the breakfast is included, be sure to place this understanding in your budget. You will not have to spend the money for breakfast each morning; therefore, that money can go to other fun things.

Also, be aware that many destinations across the world incur a daily city tax which might not be included in your hotel room rent up front. Make sure you read the hotel policy on charges and rents carefully.

Here's a list of potential additional charges you might not have planned for:

- Hotel Parking
- Wireless Internet
- Extra bedding in the room
- Breakfast
- City Tax
- Pool facilities
- Phone calls from the hotel room
- Laundry
- One-time cleaning charges at apartment
- Security fee.

To Summarize:

 Know how much money you have to spare for your vacations. Then make travel and accommodation arrangements, and not vice versa.

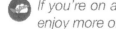 *If you're on a budget, you might need to compromise on one, to enjoy more of the other.*

 When making a trip budget, take into account international travel, accommodation, travel insurance, local travel at destination, food, entertainment, and some quota for unexpected expenses.

 Be wary of hidden fees and charges at your hotel, apartment or hostel.

Chapter 9

Last Minute Pre-Vacation Checks and Preparations

Consider Travel Insurance…

Accidents do happen. At first instance, this may seem like an unnecessary evil. But things can go wrong in the blink of an eye. At the very least, lost luggage is an all-too-familiar domain for many travelers. And although some countries like the United Kingdom will give tourists the right to use emergency room services at the hospital free of cost, don't kid yourself by thinking that every country or even, every welfare state will be as welcoming when it comes to using their health facilities. A twisted ankle in Switzerland could cost you more than 600 Euros for one trip to the emergency room! Yes, we think getting travel insurance, where premiums are quite small and insignificant in comparison, will really offer you peace of mind, at the risk of sounding clichéd.

Halt All Your Mail and Newspapers

Before leaving for your vacation, be sure to hold all your mail and newspapers so that they don't build up outside your house, alerting the world that you're not home. Newspapers accumulating on your driveway allow burglars to understand that no one is at home. If you don't want to use professional services, you can always ask a friendly neighbor to pick up your mail everyday. You should definitely alert someone in the area that you are out of town, anyway; they can keep you updated about your home, keep an eye on it, and perhaps even water your plants.

Make Copies of Your Passports and Credit Cards

In order to travel to another country, everyone in your family is required to have a passport. However, your passport is one of the most likely items to be stolen while overseas. If you have copies of your passport, credit cards, and health-insurance information in a safe location back at your accommodation, you will be able to replace the originals much more quickly. To replace your passport, you can go to your country's embassy with your passport copy, complete with your passport number and information. They can reissue your passport much more quickly, and you will not have a difficult time proving your identity.

Be sure to travel with the photocopies in your carry-on bag so as not to lose them in your undercarriage luggage. Store the photocopies in your hotel safe, if possible. Leave another set of photocopies with your trusted neighbor back home, just in case.

If you currently carry your PIN number on a piece of paper in your wallet, get out of the habit. Do not bring the number with you to Europe. If your wallet is stolen, the burglar will have a very easy time taking money off your card.

Unplug Your Home's Electrical Devices

This is a safety tactic, of course, but it also decreases your electricity bill just that tiny bit. It's the little things that count.

Check the Gas

The number one safety hazard. Make sure the gas is turned off.

Prepare Yourself for Potential Long Car Trips/Flights

Understand that travel can be the single most stressful part of your entire vacation (although we reckon, if you're prepared, it can be the most fun part), especially with young children. This book has outlined several ways to make your travel times as tearless as possible. Here are some last-minute tips to keep in mind as you head to the airport:

1. Leave Yourself Plenty of Time, and Understand Your Schedule May Falter

Because your children have different needs at different, unanticipated times, it's best to arrive at the airport early to anticipate the stops and breaks in the future. (If you're traveling long-distance via vehicle, leave early. Think of the bathroom breaks, stops for leg stretching, etc.) There are several lines once you arrive to the airport: you'll have a line to check-in, a line to check your baggage, a line through security, any food or bathroom lines, and the line to board the airplane. Children do not do well with lines, so it's best to filter them throughout several hours. Do not hit all the lines one after another.

Furthermore, do not get frustrated when things do not go according to plan. If your child simply can not wait in line anymore because he or she needs a bathroom break, you need to be understanding. Once you are on the airplane, heading to your destination, you should have a bit of time to relax.

2. Continue to Narrate the Happenings to Your Children

Make flying fun. Narrate to your child the precise happenings around them to excite them. Tell your child about the flight attendants, the pilot, the various jobs around the airport.

Continue to do this as you board and fly on the airplane. Explain to them where on the globe you'll be flying; try to mark the route to them on a map. The airplane can be rather loud and evasive; there's never enough room for anyone. Try to entertain your children with toys. Opt for a new toy from the airport, for example, that gives them a sense that this occasion is novel and exciting. Your child can relate this strange experience with a new toy.

Older children always have the blessing that is the in-flight entertainment, with tons and tons of games and movies at their behest. Most facilities will also have an on-screen interactive map tracing the route of the flight.

3. Baby Road Trip Safety

If your travels take you on a long road trip, be sure to establish car seat safety. Only seventy-five percent of all baby car seats are installed in vehicles correctly. Check your instructions once more to allow complete safety.

Furthermore, always try to drive when your baby will be sleeping— around bedtime. This will allow you to concentrate at the wheel; you will not have to distract your baby from the strangeness surrounding him or her.

Check gas. Check tires.

4. Always Have Plenty of Snacks

When your children's glucose levels drop, they let you know. They become irritable, cranky, and downright terrible to be around. This is not a devastating event you'd like to experience while you're miles above sea level. Because your children will be surrounded by an array of exciting, strange stimuli, be sure to bring plenty of familiar snacks. These snacks will not only snap your children's energy levels and moods back to place, they will also alert your children that they are safe. The proper snack can go a long way in allowing your vacation to go smoothly. And you understand: you get grouchy when you're hungry, too. Go ahead. Steal a pop tart. Your children will never know!

To Summarize:

- *Consider getting travel insurance.*
- *Make arrangements for your mail while you will be away.*
- *For safety purposes, keep copies of your passports and credits with somebody back home and in your vacation rental's safety deposit box, just in case...*
- *Unplug unnecessary electrical devices back home. Check the gas.*
- *If you're taking a flight, arrive early at the airport with kids in tow. Keep talking to them about the world of airplanes, pilots and airhostesses.*
- *If you're traveling by car, check again that your kids' car seats are buckled safely. Check gas. Check tyres.*
- *Always keep snacks handy. They are mood elevators – for the kids and for you.*
- *Bon Voyage!*

Chapter 10

Arrived at Destination! Now What?

Tips for Arrival via Airport

You've made it through the long flight. And now you have to wrestle through an unfamiliar airport with tired kids in tow, suffer through customs, and make it to your hotel or vacation apartment—all before binging on your first vacation meal. Follow these tips to allow your family's airport arrival to breeze by with cranky, nap-ready children.

• Immigration and Customs can cause anxiety for both you and your children. While you're in line, be certain to prepare everything you require to enter the country. Have all the available paperwork out: your passports, your flight information for your return, and your apartment or hotel information—just in case. Sometimes immigration officials want to understand how long you're going to be in their country and where you're going to be staying. As you wait in line, continue with similar conversations as you had with your children at your home airport. Show them the passports and explain to them precisely why they need to be assessed by the officers: the other country needs to know who they are. Explain to them who the officials are and why they must do their job.

• Turn off your cell phone. Often times, your cell phone doesn't work for calls or texts in a foreign country, anyway. But if your phone makes a noise while you're speaking with the immigrations officer, he will not be happy. Play it safe, be confident and be out of there in a jiffy. You're not doing anything wrong, so need to be apprehensive. Smile. You just want to make the process as swift as possible for your already anxious and irritated children.

• Arrive at the baggage claim before your bags do, and have your luggage tags handy. To avoid theft or misplaced luggage, arrive at your appropriate baggage claim to snag any strollers or big suitcases. Beware: oftentimes children visualize the rotating belts in the baggage claim area as an elaborate playground. Keep your children back several feet as you organize your luggage, always checking your baggage claim ticket with the number on the piece of luggage you grab, if there is any confusion. You wouldn't want to trade luggage accidentally with an innocent bystander; they probably don't want all those diapers you packed!

Tips for Arrival Via Vehicle

Your arrival to your vacation destination via your family's vehicle may be wrought with grumpy children and delays. Follow these tips for the very tail end of your journey for complete comfort.

• Prepare yourself to arrive a little late. While flights are often nailed down hour by hour on a large monitor at the airport, your car ride is wrought with the unknown. That is, perhaps, the beauty of the road trip. However, if you find yourself a few hours late due to traffic, a wrong turn, or a child throwing up in the backseat, have your hotel or apartment's number ready. You'll want to call them if and when you miss your check-in time. You'll want to avoid any fees or avoid paying for a night altogether if you arrive a day late.

• Reserve a phone card just in case. When you're driving across the country and you're running a little late for check-in, you must, of course, call your hotel—as stated above. However, it's important to understand that your cell phone service company might be a little spotty in your new area. Opt to have a phone card on your person at all times. It's the twenty-first century, sure. But there's still the occasional pay phone at your average rest stop along the road.

• Check your oil, coolant, and brake fluids. Oftentimes, long car trips can burn oil more quickly than you're used to. If the dipstick that you draw from your oil tank shows the oil line dangerously low—that is, close to the tip, you'll need to fill your tank. Your vehicle's manual should tell you what sort of oil your car accepts. The same goes for your brake fluids and your coolants. **Remember**: you'll need to take this vehicle the long road back home in just a week or so. You'll want to make sure it's in working order.

• Park your vehicle in a safe place; utilize valet service, if necessary. Oftentimes, your hotel will have a specific place to store your vehicle. Keep all the parking documents they give you, just in case. If the hotel insists on valeting your vehicle, be sure to have some cash on hand to tip the driver. Leave your vehicle running and do not take your key out of the ignition. Remove all valuables and your luggage from sight. You may not see your car again until you leave your hotel, especially if your vacation destination is a lovely, walkable city.

• Keep trash bags and personal bags because you will definitely need to dispose off junk every day. A bag of personal belongings for each of you, in addition to your kids travel packs, will help keep your things organized and within reach.

Wrestling with Your Child's Initial Jetlag

• After arriving at your hotel/ accommodation, handle your children's exhaustion with a very short nap. It's crazy, sure. Your children are tired and cranky and you've perhaps traveled halfway around the world. But once you've settled into your hotel, allow your children to nap only an hour or two. This shouldn't be too difficult; they'll be revving with adrenaline from the new environment.

• Go outside immediately after that initial nap! Seeing the sun on the other side of the world will blast your children awake. They'll be amazed at the world around them; and their bodies will immediately take to the daytime and understand that it's not time for sleep yet. Try heading to the local playground or taking a long walk before dinner. Your body will need the exercise after so long in a plane, a train or a car.

• Eat right before bed, the first two nights. At home, you may eat every evening at 7 p.m. However, one of the most frequent influences of jetlag on your children will be their hunger. If they eat right before they rest for the night, they won't awake with hunger pangs. Their bodies won't be confused about why they aren't eating at certain times because they will be full.

Utilize Your Personal Resources: Look Beyond the Internet

The internet may provide you with countless tools for your vacation - from hotel tips to restaurant recommendations. However, the internet offers nothing quite as personal as your hotel's concierge or the chef down the street. Look to personal interactions to get a feel for this new city.

• Ask your hotel's concierge for a map and ask him to show you the best areas—for both you and your children. Your concierge calls this city 'home'; therefore acknowledge that he understands the place like you would your own hometown. He can circle some great parks for children; he can tell you where you should take your run in the morning and which coffee shop on the corner has the best coffee. Allow your concierge to give you his personal opinions. He's seen many families like you waft in and out of his hotel's doorway. He'll surely understand what you like.

* Always ask the chef or server what is good that evening at their restaurant. Usually this makes them very receptive to you, even if you're a foreigner with young children. If you and your family want the real taste of the culture in which you've chosen to vacation, you should look to the real people behind the culture: the chefs, inspiring countless beautiful meals and champions of their brand of local cuisine.

* Seek a local newspaper for local events. Your concierge and a quick online search can give you a sense for what tourists often do in the city. However, a local paper—with a handy Google translate app, perhaps—may be the key to allowing you into the actual "local" culture. See what the locals are up to this weekend, be it a concert at a small, family-style restaurant or a great market in the square.

How to Improvise in the Case of Bad Weather, Illness or Unexpected Occurrences

* Leave your itinerary a little loose in case bad weather rears its ugly head. Storms may swoop in when you plan on heading to the zoo for the afternoon. Be sure to have plenty of indoor and outdoor activities in case of the unexpected, to allow your family to optimize their vacation experience. Remember, however, that little children can not do as many activities as you can on vacation. If you have a rainy day, you might find some time for a bit of rest in your hotel or apartment. Your children will need it; and you may need it more than you think. Amuse yourself inside with room service or other in-house facilities like a pool, a gym or

a children's play club. After all, a vacation should leave time for rest and relaxation. Trotting isn't the only component.

• A sick kid on vacation: be prepared prior to embarking. If you're traveling to a different country, be sure to understand that your children's normal medicines may not be found there. Bring plenty to spare in your undercarriage luggage. For light fevers, look to something that will reduce the fever and keep your kids slow but moving. In case of an emergency, please remember to utilize the country's emergency code number. Ask your hotel's concierge for a local doctor's number; always have your insurance cards ready.

• You are not happy with your hotel. What to do? Be sure to check your hotel's policy. Do they offer refunds for the days you plan on not staying there? Will you have to pay extra in order to check-out early? When asking questions at your hotel's front desk, be sure to be as courteous as possible. You are asking them to go out of their way for you to pay less to the hotel. Also, be sure to check if there is another hotel that you like, with the dates you require, available. Remember: your hotel stay does not have to take up the majority of your trip. If you hate your accommodations but can "tolerate" them, you can spend as much time outside the hotel as you like.

• Remember: stay positive. Things go wrong on vacation. Your car might break down on the way to the hotel, you may get caught in the world's greatest traffic jam, or your youngest might throw up all over your new coat. You are a parent. Innovation and improvisation are a part of your life. You want your vacation to be an escape from your real life, but you aren't escaping the requirements of parenting. Care for your children in all manners first. Improvise to make them comfortable and safe. When everything falls into place, head to the museum. (Promise ice cream for afterwards.)

• Click away! Avoid fake smiles some of the times. The posed picture of your family in front of the great gothic castle in Europe may be the one you choose for your mantel. But it doesn't capture the true feeling of your vacation. Be sure to take as many "action" shots of your family as possible: your child riding the horse at the park and laughing, your spouse mid-spaghetti bite... These are natural moments that encapsulate the beauty of your vacation together; they also position the members of your family

Chapter 11

And It's a Wrap!

How to Make the Most of Your Last Evening on Vacation

• Your last evening is the last evening of a priceless adventure. Make it special for everyone by choosing a restaurant or a special place where everyone can come together comfortably and happily. Remember: this does not always mean you head to the ritzy Italian place with candles and the best bruschetta in town. If your children are happiest at the pizza parlor down the street, you may find yourself feeling happiest there as well. It's the end of a vacation, and everyone's tired. Take this opportunity to commune as a family one last time, before you return to routine.

• Ask your children to engage with you by revealing their favorite parts of the vacation. **Ask them their favorite foods, their favorite parks, or what they like most about the hotel. If they are old enough, ask them to write their memories down for you. Allow them to understand that writing their experiences and adventures allows them to keep the memories for much longer. When you arrive back to your home and back to your schedules, you and your children will be able to look back on what they wrote and reminisce. Writing is a great, though sadly, under-rated memorabilia.**

Tips for Packing for Home

• Keep the dirty clothes separate. **Wrap your children's dirty clothes tightly in trash bag or plastic bag found in your hotel room or apartment. This will allow easy distribution to the washing machine upon your arrival home.**

• Be sure not to fly with meat, vegetables, or fruit.

• You must declare all items you bring back to your country after flying home. **Each country is different on the amount of things you can bring back with you. In the United States, for example, each child and adult can bring up to $1,600 worth of items back to his country. Many other**

countries range in the $800 area.

- Do not pack valuables in a shopping bag. Opt to buy bubble wrap and position them safely in your carryon. If you place valuables in the shopping bag you received them in, meaning to bring them all the way back home with you, think again. Many things are broken or damaged in the overhead compartments of airplanes.

Tips for Your Flight Home

- If possible, arrive at the airport the same way you left from the airport when you first came. This way, you'll already understand the process. Taxi services can be found via your hotel concierge or online.

Be sure to explain to your children that you'll be going through similar processes for similar reasons. They've gone through this airport and the airport at home before. Allow them to choose an item from the airport snack shop after security check. Remind them that they'll receive a snack of their choice if they are good through check-in and security. This might also help a bit with the sadness of a glorious vacation having come to an end, with novelty and excitement.

- Remember to keep the copies of your passport/credit card/important documents in your carry-on bag. Bad things happen in airports all the time. If your passport is stolen at the airport prior to boarding your airplane, you'll have the important documents you need in copy form. Tell either your flight's company or an airport security member immediately; show them your documents.

Tips for Your Long Drive Back Home

- Check the car oil and fuel once more prior to embarking back home. Check your oil, your brake fluid, and your coolant as you did upon your arrival. You'll want to ensure your car is in proper working order.

- Pack a special bag for each of your children featuring games and toys that he/she likes. Adding novelty to your trip allows your child to feel excited—not anxious, unsure, and downright bored. If you show your child a way to stay active with him or herself in the backseat, he/she won't be bothering you constantly about how long you've been on the road.

Remember to stop consistently. With young children, a good pattern lies in two hours on the road with a twenty-minute stop. Understand that your children need time to stretch their legs. During restaurant stops, try to find restaurants with play places. Play places allow your children to rattle around and explore and stretch their legs; beyond that, they allow you to rest and refuel without answering a million questions or complaints, from a child who never wanted the vacation to come to an end.

Back to the Daily Grind: How to Assimilate to "Real" Life Once More

You planned your vacation for weeks and weeks. You explored a different world; you showed your children new, exciting things; and you hit a few pitfalls along the way. All in all, your vacation was a great success. And now you must return. How can you assimilate yourselves back to life at home?

- Commit to the anti-jetlag routine as suggested above. Engage in one short nap after your return and then hit the streets or some indoor activities, if it's still daytime outside. Take your children to their favorite playground, go for a long walk, and assimilate to the everyday surroundings. Remember to eat right before you go to bed to avoid middle of the night hunger pangs. Your children may want to sleep at bizarre times; don't let them.

- Try to arrive home at least a few days before office and school schedules resume. Give yourself a few days to recuperate from your vacation and loosen yourself from the nags of fatigue and a jetlag. Do your laundry, unpack your new knick-knacks, and unwind in front of the television. Make your children their favorite foods. But stick to the eating and sleeping schedule that you'll need in the next few days when work and school kick in. Don't give in to a sleepy head easily!

- Call your co-workers to see what has occurred while you've been out of town. Your first day back at work can be jarring. Commit to a smooth morning back by calling a few of your close co-workers to catch up. Make a list of all the things you need to complete in the first morning you're back at work. If you have the tasks running already in your mind, you won't find your first day back so rough.

- Make a play date for your children. If your children feel a little strange coming back home after all the excitement, allow them to hook up with a few of their old friends. They'll enjoy narrating holiday stories to friends, and gradually, settle back into the routine social norms. School can then follow.

- Turn your mail back on or retrieve your mail from your neighbor. Hopefully you've been responsible with your mail and not allowed it to build up in your mailbox. Alert your post office that you can begin receiving mail again or thank your neighbor for keeping your home safe. Did you get him a gift?

- Attend to your electrical items. You've limited your electricity bill by unplugging your lamps and televisions and speakers, etc. Restore your home to its old self.

Leave Time for Reminiscing and Create a Family Photo Album

- After a few days at home, gather your family together. You're back to your old life; you're running around pell-mell with a million things to do once more. It was the very life you chose to escape for that week of family fun. Reminisce together a few days after you return in order to restore the magic you all once felt and remind yourselves that these beautifully nostalgic, after-vacation days were all a result of a lovely trip.

- Gather your children's written memories, your photographs, any trinkets or postcards together and make a family photo album. Twenty years down the line, you'll adore your chunky-cheeked child's grin on the carousel. You'll love your child's every written memory down to the last misspelled word. Creating the photo album will allow you time to re-live the memories in the midst of your work and hectic adult life. Make a rich, inclusive family photo album that you all can appreciate for all times to come.

Share your Travel Experiences with Other Parents

- There is a definite kick to be had, in 'giving back' to the world. Other parents would love to hear about your travels, and all the tips, tricks and suggestions that you might have to offer. The forums at www.theflyingkids.com await you!

Conclusion

We hope that our All-Inclusive Guide to Traveling and Vacationing with Children allows you to understand your children's vacation desires and needs. It teaches you to place your travel expectations a bit lower: things won't get done as quickly, remember, and you probably won't go to all the museums you'd like to see. Your schedule must be fluid, flexible, while also keeping everyone's needs and desires in mind. It seems exhausting. Furthermore, you understand the things you need to do prior to shipping off to your destination: copies of your passport are a must, for example, as is dealing with your mail. You must arm your children with all that they need, in order to avoid vacation disruption: carefully sway them from culture shock by alerting them to differences beforehand, allowing them to become excited by the strangeness of the world.

Vacationing is a great deal of work. But when your children are happy, smiling, and experiencing the magic of travel with you, you will soon start making plans for the next big vacation! Travel is a great gift. A gift of adventure and education.

Appendix:

Itinerary Template

Day A: Destination 1 – Destination 2 – Destination 3 - ...

Scheduled time slots	Destination/ attraction	How to get there	Things to take into account	Comments

CPSIA information can be obtained at www.ICGtesting.com
Printed in the USA
LVOW10s0921070615

441502LV00019B/1070/P

9 781500 381080